A Thank You

I want to say Thank You for buying a free gift for you!

This gift is the perfect complement to this book so just visit the link below to get access.

www.GoodLivingPublishing.com/6packchef

Hope you like your free gift.

Contents

Introduction 5

9 Rules for Getting Shredded 8

The Recipes 14

Breakfast Recipes 15

    Smokey Mackerel Omelette 16

    English Breakfast Kippers 17

    Mexican Omelette 18

    Protein Packed Oatmeal 19

    Chorizo Toast & Tomato 20

    Honey & Fruit Granola 21

    Breakfast Burrito 22

    Baked Avocado 23

    Protein Packed Pancakes 24

    Cottage Cheese Pot 25

    Spicy Scrambled 26

    Egg n Bacon Cups 27

    Bacon Avocado Omelette 28

    Huevos Rancheros 29

    Stuffed Tomatoes 30

    Veggie Pita 31

Breakfast Smoothies 32

    Strawberry & Coconut Delight 33

    The Banana Whey 34

    Morning Rise 35

    Berry Storm 36

    Mango Muchness 37

Lunch Recipes 38
   Shrimp Stir Fry 39
   The Chicken Power Fajita 40
   Tuna Stuffed Pita 41
   Chickpea & Bean Salad 42
   Hot Soup 43
   90 second Tuna Lunch 44
   Spiced Steak Strips 45
   Feta & Nut Salad 46
   Bean Burrito 47
   Eggs in Purgatory 48
   Spiced Sausage & Bean Soup 49
   Spicy, Roasted Chicken Tenders 51
   Mackerel & Beetroot Salad 52
   Green and Mean Salad 54
   Nicoise Salad 55
   Tuna Stir Fry 56

Dinner Recipes 57
   Scallop & Vegetable Kabobs 58
   Beef Chilli Verde 59
   Quinoa 61
   Mediterranean Inspired Chicken 62
   Lean Chilli 63
   Chilli Baked Salmon 65
   Jerk Seasoned Chicken 66
   Turkey Meatball Chilli 67
   Seafood Linguine 69
   Protein Paella 70

- Steak Salad 72
- Veggie Burger 73
- Garlic Baked Tilapia 74
- Honey Ginger Salmon 75
- Flaked Fish in Lemon Lentils 76
- Rosemary & Garlic Chicken 78

Sides Recipes 79
- Cauliflower Mash 80
- Greens for Any Dish 81
- Need More Carbs? 82
- Baked Sweet Potato 83
- Stuffed Mushrooms 84
- Kale Chips 85

Introduction

Hey,

Thanks for buying "The 6 Pack Chef" I know you're going to love this book, and more importantly your new chiselled abs.

I wrote this book because there is so much nonsense in the fitness industry (especially concerning 6 packs) that trying to distinguish what works and what doesn't is hellish. This book is the solution to that pain.

The 6 Pack Chef is a collection of the best 6 packs rules and recipes that I have provided for my clients over my time as a personal trainer. The results my clients have seen are staggering and I've only had 1 client who didn't reach his body fat % goals. He was a 21 year old college kid who wasn't willing to give up us his 3 – 4 nights of partying a week.

Before you dive into this book there are a few points I want to touch upon to get you primed and ready.

1. You will need to exercise, it simply isn't possible to be lean (combination of muscle and low body fat) without exercise. You do NOT need to be a member of a gym, but I do highly recommend it.

2. A shredded midsection appears when you get to 9-12% body fat. Following this book will get you there. However if you want to drop to a "competition" level of body fat, usually around 4-7% then you will need to follow more advance techniques. Some techniques could be Intermittent Fasting, counting your macros, water weight manipulation and many others.

3. As you go through the recipes you will notice ingredients popping up again and again. There are reasons these

commons ingredient have been chosen and the reasons are to aid you in your goals.

4. You will notice that I do not suggest the common 5-6 small meals per day. Instead I recommend 3 meals per day split into the usual Breakfast, Lunch and Dinner. Why do I recommend this? Well, I say it for a few reasons firstly being that 5-6 small meals per day does NOT promote more fat loss – this is a myth.

    It is simply "bro-science" but thankfully some real scientists in both France and Canada decided to test the 5-6 meals a day theory and guess what they found? Yup, they found that there is "no evidence of improved weight loss" by eating frequent small meals. They even went further into the research and found that there was no difference between grazing and gorging.

    The biggest benefit you get from the results of this research is that you are no longer having to constantly take time out of your busy schedule to eat. Just eat at the usual times: breakfast, lunch and dinner.

5. In relation to point 4, the one thing you must do is ensure you eat within 45 minutes after a workout. Always eat a post workout meal and ensure it has a mixture of protein, carbohydrates and fat. Breakfast is not the most important meal of the day… post gym meal is the most important.

6. Counting calories isn't necessary. I will say that again… Counting your calories is not needed in order to get lean, all you need to do is ensure you are eating less than you are expending. Remember, your resting metabolic rate of caloric burn will be around the 2000 – 2400 - that is the calories you will burn if you were to do nothing but lie in bed all day. So by exercising regularly you will be burning more. What this means is that you don't need to be focused on the number of calories you eat…

Instead focus on the QUALITY of calories you eat. Ensure you eat whole, natural foods and strictly limit (or eliminate) sugars, additives etc. this will be much more effective, easier to stick to and give you accelerated results. Every recipe and portion size in the book is in line with this logic, so just follow the recipes and make your own adjustments with the side dishes if needed (your body will tell you what it needs).

So, dive into the book now and explore the delicious recipes I've put together for you. Every recipe is simple to cook and delivers the combination of nutrients that your body needs to strip away fat and reveal your 6 pack.

Read the 9 Rules for Getting Shredded before you start cooking as it will shine more light on some of the dietary choices you are going to be making.

Happy cooking.

Peter

P.S Don't forget to check out the Free Gift you get for buying. It's the perfect complement to this book.

9 Rules for Getting Shredded

This section will explore the various rules you have to follow in order to shred off fat and reveal your 6 pack. These rules are simple to follow and you will most likely have come across some of them before.

Read them carefully and follow them religiously.

The first few rules are all set around the famous (and very true) saying of "Abs are made in the kitchen, not the gym."

The key to getting truly shredded is through the correct approach to diet. So without further ado, here are the rules for getting shredded.

1 – You Have to Eat.

If you want to be lean and have a shredded 6 pack you have to eat. Starving yourself will just result in a loss of muscle, a screwed up metabolism and a malnourished appearance. By eating you will be providing your body will everything it needs to burn fat, keep your metabolism working, feed your muscles and ultimately get shredded – but remember you need to eat the right foods, which brings us to rule 2.

2 – Eat the Right Foods

Unless you are a freak of nature or on steroids you won't be able to get shredded by eating whatever you like. You need to base your diet around whole foods and avoiding manufactured/processed foods. (Check out your free gift for a shopping list of foods)

Whole foods can be considered anything that isn't packed full of additives and came out of a factory. Sure the packet of cooked chicken at the grocery store might boast 30g of protein but look closer at the nutritional info and you will see a long list of additives – these will prevent you ever getting truly lean.

Conversely, eating natural whole foods (nuts, grass-fed beef, organic chicken, eggs, beans, legumes etc.) will give your body the nutrients it requires to burn the stubborn fat hiding your abs.

Going 100% natural can be very difficult and is not essential, instead you should aim for 80% whole-foods. This means you can still eat (in small doses) things like hot sauces, certain breads etc. This 80/20 split will help you stick to your diet, not go crazy, prevent cravings and save you money.

3 – Every Meal Must Have a Protein Source

Being shredded is not just about losing body fat, you also need to have a substantial amount of muscle. Lean muscle burns fat, the more muscle you have the more fat you burn and the building block of muscle is protein.

When you are on the quest to reveal your abs you will be in a calorie deficit (expending more calories than you take in) and when in a deficit protein will carry out the following functions:

- Keep you feeling fuller longer as protein aids satiety and prevents hunger
- Prevent muscle breakdown from calorie reduction

Ensuring you have protein with every meal combined with a weight lifting routine (rule 6) will carve out a 6 pack very quickly.

4 – Eat Greens & Keep Fibre High

The fibre you get from green vegetables and carbs such as legumes have some excellent health benefits which make them essential for getting shredded. Eating more fibre has been proven to help you control weight fluctuations, lose weight quicker, promote a healthier heart and increase your levels of satiety after a meal. Aim to eat some greens and fibre in every meal. As you go through the recipes in this book you will notice how many of them call for these ingredients.

5- Don't Be Afraid of Fat

It seems counter intuitive but eating fat helps you lose fat. Your body requires fat to function, it's a crucial building block, and ensuring you consume dietary fat will help you reach your goals faster. The main foods you want to derive your fats from are things like extra-virgin olive oil, steak, beef, chicken thighs and avocado.

If you limit your fat intake too steeply then your body will go into "survival mode" and not let go of its existing fat stores as it is concerned no more is coming. Avoid this by accepting healthy dietary fats as an essential part of your diet.

6 - Lift Weights

If you want to reveal your abs you need to lift weights. As mentioned in the previous rule muscle burns fat but there are other reasons you need to lift if you want to reveal your 6 pack:

- Lifting weights is highly metabolic and torches fat
- Increases testosterone – higher T levels are directly linked to an increase in fat burning
- To build muscle, strength the core and increase the size of abdominal muscles

Create a workout focused around heavy weights and compound movements such as squats, deadlifts and the bench press. Ensure you give your muscles ample time to recover and don't over train.

7- Do Strategic High Intensity Cardio 1-2x Per Week

In order to get to sub 10% body fat you will need to do some form of cardiovascular activity in addition to your weight lifting routine.

The most effective cardio you can do is referred to as High Intensity Interval Training (HIIT). This style of training requires you to do very intense short bursts of exercise followed by a short rest period, repeated several times. A Common HIIT protocol would consist of sprinting at 80% of your max speed for 30 seconds followed by 30 seconds of rest before repeating 6-8 times.

The benefits of HIIT over steady state cardio are listed below:

- You will burn more fat and continue burning fat for up to 24 hours after the routine
- It targets fat, not muscle

- Stimulates testosterone and HGH production in a massive way
- Increase in lung capacity and strength
- It's over in around 10 minutes

HIIT is very difficult but the rewards are worth it. You can use any form of cardio machine to do it and if you Google HIIT routines or Tabata Training you will find excellent routines to follow. Stick to it and you will see incredible results, and always remember it may be difficult – but it's over quickly.

8 – Train Fasted (if possible)

If your schedule allows for it train early in the morning in a fasted state. Fasted state training has a plethora of benefits which will allow you to carve out your abs at an accelerated pace. The benefits of training early in the morning are shown below:

- Your testosterone levels are at their highest in the morning
- You prime your body to burn fat for the remainder of the day
- Any food you eat after working out will go straight to your muscles and not have the opportunity to turn to fat

The benefits of training fasted will now be listed:

- Increase in production of HGH (human growth hormone)
- Your body targets fat cells for energy as no food is available for fuel
- You will NOT have an insulin spike

The first few times you train fasted will feel unusual but by the 3rd or 4th session you will notice an increase in energy levels and performance in the gym. I recommended a large black coffee or double espresso (no sugar, cream etc.) before the gym to help with your energy levels.

Ensure you eat as soon as possible after your workout.

9 – Refuel Every 7-10 Days

In order to strip away body fat and reveal your abs it is essential that you are in a caloric deficit the majority of the time. However it is also crucial that you 'refuel' every so often. A refuel day consists of greatly spiking your caloric intake in order to achieve the following:

- Reset your leptin levels
- Boosts your metabolism
- Replenish your glycogen stores
- Stop you losing your mind when cutting

A refuel day is very important to anyone wanting to reveal their abs, but several things should be noted about the day. Do not confuse it with a 'cheat day' you will still be eating the same healthy foods, just in greater amounts. Do not eat for the sake of eating, just eat more each meal. If you need to eat something sweet for the sake of your sanity, be very careful with the portion control.

Plan your refuel days ahead of time, decide what you are going to eat ahead of time and make sure you enjoy the feeling of the increase protein, carbs and fats pulsing through your body.

The Recipes

The recipes in this book are under the titles of Breakfast, Lunch and Dinner but by no means does this mean they should only be eaten at this time. I simply put them under these headings as a guideline. Feel free to switch it up however you like.

Every recipe is specifically designed to aid you in getting shredded and revealing your abs. The combination of foods and the serving size make each recipe perfect for those looking to lose fat without jeopardizing muscle.

Before you dive into the recipes I want to mention a few things.

- If a recipe does not tell you what to serve the food with just check out the "Sides Recipes" section and choose one of those.
- Your post workout meal is the most important meal and I would always ensure it has a form of carbohydrates in it. If the recipe you choose doesn't have carbs, go check out the "Sides Recipes" again and throw in a carb choice.
- The smoothie section calls for specific flavours of protein powder to be used, however if you have a different flavoured protein powder, don't let this stop you. Just throw it in and the taste will still be amazing.
- If your body tells you it needs more food add either an extra portion of carbs to one meal a day (post workout is best) or increase the amount of greens you eat. Common signs that your body needs more are: loss of muscle, huge loss of energy (not just being slightly tired) and hunger headaches (very uncommon).

Breakfast Recipes

Smokey Mackerel Omelette

Ingredients

Spinach, 1 pressed cup

Smoked mackerel fillet

4 eggs

1 tablespoon extra-virgin olive oil

Ground pepper, to taste

Directions

Heat broiler/grill.

Place a pan over a medium heat and add oil.

Tear or cut spinach into pieces and add to pan and cook for 1 minute, or until spinach is wilted.

Flake the mackerel fillet into the pan and heat for 1-2 minutes.

In a bowl whisk together the eggs and some pepper. Add the spinach and mackerel and mix well.

Pour mixture into the pan from previous step and cook at a low-medium heat for 5-6 minutes. The middle should still be runny but the edges should be browning.

Once this stage is reached place the full pan under the grill/broiler and cook for 1-2 minutes.

English Breakfast Kippers

Ingredients

2 eggs

2 fillets of smoked kippers

1.5 cups of spinach, pressed

1 slice of toast, whole-wheat, gluten-free, rye or multigrain

1 tablespoon extra-virgin olive oil

Black pepper to taste

Cayenne pepper to taste

Directions

In a pot add water and bring close to the boil.

Turn the heat down and swirl the water with a fork. Carefully add the eggs to the swirling water and let poach for 2-3 minutes.

Spoon out the poached eggs and set aside carefully.

Place a pan over a medium heat and add the oil.

Add the kippers and spinach, cook for 2 minutes. As they are cooking toast your bread.

Once the bread is toasted layer it with the spinach and kippers before setting the poached egg atop.

Sprinkle with black pepper and cayenne pepper to taste.

Mexican Omelette

Ingredients

3 eggs

Medium or Hot Salsa

Ground paprika, to taste

1 tablespoon extra-virgin olive oil

½ cup spinach, pressed

Ground pepper, to taste

Directions

Place a pan over a medium heat and add the olive oil.

Whist the oil heats whisk the eggs, pepper and paprika in a bowl.

Pour the egg into the pan and leave to cook for 2-3 minutes.

Once the egg begins to set in the middle add the spinach to one half of the omelette.

Add the salsa on top of the spinach and fold the empty half of the omelette onto the filling.

Let cook for a further 2-3 minutes.

Protein Packed Oatmeal

Ingredients

¾ cup of oatmeal, quick cook oats are easiest

1 tablespoon peanut butter, natural

1 scoop of chocolate protein powder

Directions

Add the oatmeal to a bowl and cover with water.

Microwave until oats are ready, stirring once or twice during cooking.

Add the peanut butter, protein powder and an additional 2 tablespoons of water. Stir well until fully mixed.

If needed microwave for a further 15-20 seconds.

Chorizo Toast & Tomato

Ingredients

2 large tomatoes, chopped

1 tablespoon of butter, unsalted

Chorizo sausage, from a sausage cut 4 round slices

½ teaspoon Hot pepper flakes

1 slice toast, whole-wheat, rye, multigrain or gluten-free

Directions

In a bowl mix together the sausage, pepper, chopped tomatoes. Toss well

Start toasting your bread.

Microwave the sausage and tomato mixture for 1 minute

Remove from microwave and add butter. Toss well.

Spoon the mixture onto the toast.

Honey & Fruit Granola

Ingredients

1 cup granola

½ cup mixed fruit

2 tablespoons honey

2 tablespoons fat free yoghurt

Directions

Cook the granola according to the package instructions, or eat cold

Add the mixed fruit and honey. Stir well.

Spoon the yoghurt over the top.

Breakfast Burrito

Ingredients

2 eggs, whisked

2 large tomatoes, chopped

1 red onion, sliced

1 jalapeno pepper, sliced

1 teaspoon minced garlic, or finely chopped

1 Wholemeal tortilla

1 tablespoon extra-virgin olive oil

2 tablespoons hot salsa

Cheese, cheddar

Directions

Place a pan over a medium heat and add the oil.

Once heated throw in the onion, garlic and pepper. Cook for 2-3 minutes.

Add the whisked eggs and scramble until almost cooked.

Add the tomatoes and hot salsa. Cook for a further 1-2 minutes.

Take off the heat and sprinkle the cheese over the top. Fold once.

Spoon into your tortilla and wrap up into a burrito.

Baked Avocado

Ingredients

1 Avocado

1 teaspoon extra-virgin olive oil

Ground cayenne pepper, to taste

Directions

Preheat oven to 350F

Half avocado and remove the stone.

Slice the underside of each avocado to create a flat surface.

Rest avocado on baking tray, the hole from stone should be visible.

Drizzle oil over the avocado halves and sprinkle with cayenne.

Bake for 10-15 minutes.

Protein Packed Pancakes

Ingredients

½ cup quick oats

½ cup cottage cheese, use low-fat

3 eggs, whites only

3 tablespoons protein powder, banana flavour is delicious as is chocolate.

Handful of blueberries

2 teaspoons maple syrup

1 tablespoon extra-virgin olive oil

Directions

In a food processor or using hand blender mix together the oats, cheese, egg whites and protein powder until it resembles a pancake batter. If it becomes too thick, add water 1 tablespoon at a time.

Heat the oil in a pan over a medium heat.

Pour in the batter and let it cook for around 3 minutes per side.

Remove from pan and serve with blueberries and maple syrup (both are optional)

Cottage Cheese Pot

Ingredients

¾ cup of cottage cheese, low fat

1 scoop chocolate protein powder

½ cup mixed fruit

1 tablespoon honey

Directions

Combine all ingredients in a bowl and mix well.

Spicy Scrambled

Ingredients

3 eggs, whisked

½ tin of kidney beans, drained

1 large chopped tomato

Ground cayenne pepper, to taste

Ground paprika, to taste

1 tablespoon extra-virgin olive oil

1 tablespoon hot salsa, optional

Directions

Place a pot over a medium heat and add the kidney beans, chopped tomato, paprika and cayenne. Mix well and warm through.

Place a pan over a medium heat and add the oil.

Add the eggs to the pan and begin to scramble. After 1 minute of cooking add the contents of the pot and toss well cook for 1 minute.

The eggs should be close to finished now so turn off the heat and add the salsa. Mix well.

Leave off the heat for a minute to finish cooking the eggs.

Egg n Bacon Cups

Ingredients

6 eggs

6 slices bacon

Sea salt, to taste

Ground pepper, to taste

Directions

Preheat your oven to 350F.

Take a muffin pan and line the muffin holes with bacon. Press the meat around the sides of the hole but not across the bottom.

Add one cracked egg into each hole and add salt and pepper.

Bake in oven for 18 minutes. The bacon should be crispy and the egg should be set.

They will pop right out of the tin.

Bacon Avocado Omelette

Ingredients

3 eggs, whisked

3 rashers of bacon

1 avocado, stoned removed, skinned and chopped into chunks. You will only be using half.

½ red onion, finely chopped

Cilantro, finely chopped, around 1 teaspoon worth

Hot sauce, to taste

Directions

Cook bacon under the grill/broiler or in a pan.

As bacon cooks take your avocado chunks and add to a bowl. Mash the avocado slightly with a fork.

Add the onion and cilantro to the bowl and mix well.

Once bacon is cooked cut it up and throw it in the bowl as well. Mix again.

In a greased pan over a medium heat add the eggs and leave to cook for 2 minutes.

Once the omelette begins to form and the middle isn't runny anymore scoop the avocado mixture onto one half of the omelette.

Fold the empty half over the avocado mix to complete the omelette.

Cook until ready.

Huevos Rancheros

Ingredients

½ cup of black beans

2 eggs

1 tablespoon extra-virgin olive oil

2 tablespoons grated reduced fat cheddar

¼ cup of medium/hot salsa

Directions

Place a pan over a medium heat and add the oil.

Add the black beans and salsa once the oil has been heated and stir well.

Cook for 3 minutes stirring frequently.

Move the black beans and salsa to one side of the pan, clearing a space for the eggs.

Crack the two eggs in the pan and fry until cooked sunny side up.

Sprinkle the cheese over the black beans.

Serve with the eggs laid over the black bean and salsa mixture.

Stuffed Tomatoes

Ingredients

2 Large tomatoes, tops cut off and inside scooped out.

2 rashers of bacon

Ground paprika, to taste

Sea salt, to taste

Directions

Preheat oven to 350F

Cook the bacon under a grill/broiler and once cooked remove and tear into small pieces.

Add the scooped tomato and bacon to a bowl along with paprika and mix well.

Spoon the mixture into the tomatoes and set on a baking tray.

Bake for 10-15 minutes.

Sprinkle salt to taste.

Veggie Pita

Ingredients

1 whole-wheat pita

4 tablespoons hummus

1 large tomato, sliced

1 oz. crumbled goat's cheese

¼ cup sliced almonds

Directions

In a bowl mix together all the ingredients except for the pita.

Microwave for 30 – 60 seconds.

Stuff the pita with filling and either eat cold or bake in oven for 10 minutes.

Breakfast Smoothies

Strawberry & Coconut Delight

Ingredients

1.5 cups of strawberries, around 8-10 strawberries

½ cup plain fat free yoghurt, you can also use vanilla flavour

1 scoop protein powder, strawberry or vanilla

½ cup shredded coconut.

Directions

Blend until smooth

The Banana Whey

Ingredients

2 bananas

½ cup vanilla flavoured yoghurt, fat free

1 scoop whey protein powder, vanilla or chocolate

Directions

Blend until smooth.

Morning Rise

Ingredients

½ cup chilled green tea, or 2 teaspoons green tea powder

½ cup vanilla soymilk

Handful of blueberries

1 scoop protein powder

½ cup vanilla flavoured yoghurt

Directions

Blend until smooth.

Berry Storm

Ingredients

Handful of cranberries

Handful of blueberries

Handful strawberries

½ cup vanilla flavoured yoghurt

1 scoop protein powder

Directions

Blend until smooth

Mango Muchness

Ingredients

½ mango, skinned

2 peaches, stones removed

Handful of strawberries

½ cup vanilla flavoured frozen yoghurt

Directions

Blend until smooth.

Lunch Recipes

Shrimp Stir Fry

Ingredients

2 teaspoons garlic, minced or finely chopped

½ teaspoon ginger, ground or minced

3 Spring onions, chopped

Pak choi, torn

1 cup of king prawns, raw

1 bag of beansprouts

2 tablespoons soy sauce

Half of a lemon, juiced

Sesame seeds

1 tablespoon extra-virgin olive oil

Directions

Place a wok over a medium heat and add the oil.

Once oil is heated add the garlic, onion and ginger. Cook for 2 minutes, stirring continually.

Throw the prawns in the pan and cook for 30 seconds, stirring continually.

Add the pak choi and bean sprouts and cook for 1 minute. Stirring frequently.

Once the prawns turn pink (a sign they are almost done) add the soy sauce, lemon juice and a generous amount of sesame seeds.

Toss well and cook until the prawns are cooked fully.

The Chicken Power Fajita

Ingredients

1 Chicken breast, cut into thin slices

1 bell pepper, sliced

1 red onion, sliced

Lemon zest

¼ Cottage cheese

1 Wholemeal tortilla

1 tablespoon extra-virgin oil

Directions

Place a pan over a medium heat with olive oil.

Once heated add the onion, pepper and chicken to the pan and cook for 8-10 minutes. Stirring frequently.

Once the chicken is cooked take off the heat and add the lemon zest and cottage cheese. Toss well.

Spoon the chicken onto the tortilla and wrap.

Tuna Stuffed Pita

Ingredients

1 tin of tuna

1 red onion, sliced

1 teaspoon minced garlic, or finely chopped

Hot sauce, to taste

1.5 tablespoons low fat mayonnaise

Directions

Preheat oven to 325F.

In a bowl add the onion, garlic, tuna and mayonnaise together. Mix well. Microwave for 1 minute, stirring half way through.

Add hot sauce and stir well.

Open pita and stuff tuna filling inside.

Cook for 15-20 minutes.

Chickpea & Bean Salad

Ingredients

2 cups green beans, chopped

1 can of chickpeas, drained

1 can of black beans, drained

1 bell pepper, sliced

1 handful walnuts

1 onions, sliced

¼ cup chopped coriander

2 tablespoons extra-virgin olive oil

Ground black pepper, to taste

Juice from half of a lime

Directions

Add the green beans to a microwave safe bowl, add an inch of water and cover.

Microwave for 2 minutes, or until cooked.

In a large bowl add all the ingredients and drizzle with extra-virgin olive oil. Toss well.

Plate up and drizzle lime juice and add pepper to taste.

Hot Soup

Ingredients

250g noodles, rice noodles are best

5 cups chicken stock

1 red chilli, cut into thin strips

Fresh ginger, cut into thin matchsticks about an inch long each

1 tablespoon light soy sauce

Juice squeezed from 1 lime

1 Salmon fillet, torn into pieces

1 peeled carrot, grated

1 courgette, grated

Directions

Cook the noodles according to pack instructions

In a pot over a medium heat add the stock, chilli and ginger. Bring to the boil.

Let simmer for 2 minutes before stirring in the soy sauce and lime juice.

Add the noodles and salmon and cook for 2 minutes.

Add the carrot and courgette and cook for a further 2 minutes.

Take off heat and let sit for 1-2 minutes.

90 second Tuna Lunch

Ingredients

1 can of tuna

1 tin of kidney beans, drained

1 teaspoon red pepper flakes

1 teaspoon paprika

¼ cup of hot salsa

Directions

Mix all ingredients in a microwave proof bowl and cook for 90 seconds.

Spiced Steak Strips

Ingredients

1 steak, any cut will do but avoid the thicker cuts such as fillet

3 tablespoons tomato paste or puree

2 tablespoons paprika

2 teaspoons red pepper flakes

2 tablespoons extra-virgin olive oil

Ground black pepper, to taste

1 slice of bread, toasted. Gluten free, multigrain, rye or whole-wheat

1 tablespoon of butter, unsalted

Directions

Cut steak into thin slices and add to a bowl.

Add tomato paste, paprika, pepper flakes, pepper and toss well.

Place a pan over a high heat and add the olive oil.

Wait until the pan has reached a very high heat before adding the meat.

Cook for 3 minutes, stirring constantly to avoid it sticking to the pan.

Take off the heat and leave in the pan.

Toast the bread and spread butter.

Spoon steak onto the bread.

Feta & Nut Salad

Ingredients

¼ cup of feta cheese, crumbled or torn

Handful of watercress, chopped

Handful of salad leaves

8 Cherry tomatoes, halved

1.5 tablespoons red wine vinegar

Handful of walnuts

Ground black pepper, to taste

Sea salt, to taste

Directions

In a large bowl add all the ingredients and toss well.

Season with salt and pepper

Bean Burrito

Ingredients

1 can of black beans, drained

3 tablespoons tomato paste

Ground paprika, to taste

Ground cayenne, to taste

1 whole-wheat tortilla

1 cup of shredded lettuce

¼ cup hot salsa

Directions

Add the shredded lettuce to a pot of water and bring to the boil.

Cover and let simmer until cooked, 5 minutes or so. Drain once cooked.

Place a pan over a medium heat and add the black beans, tomato paste, paprika, cayenne and salsa. Mix well and stir frequently.

Cook for 5 minutes.

Warm the tortilla in the microwave for 10 seconds.

Add the lettuce and black bean mix to the tortilla and wrap up

Eggs in Purgatory

3 large eggs

1 bunch of asparagus, chopped (remove the ends and dispose)

¾ cups marinara sauce

1 tablespoon olive oil

1 clove garlic, finely chopped

1 cup chicken broth

Directions

Put a large pan over a medium heat and add the olive oil. As the oil begins to heat add the garlic and cook until slightly brown. Should take 1-2 minutes.

Pour in the marinara sauce and then the chicken broth, stir well.

Add asparagus pieces, stir and then cover the pan until the sauce begins to boil.

When the sauce boils reduce the heat to low. Gently crack your eggs you eggs and add on top of sauce. Just as if you were making a fried egg.

Simmer on low for 10 minutes

Spiced Sausage & Bean Soup

This recipe makes enough for 4 servings. It can be kept in fridge for up to a week.

Ingredients

½ pound of Italian sausage

1 onion chopped finely

1 tbsp garlic, minced

2 tbsp olive oil

1 can cannellini beans

6 cups gluten-free chicken stock

Hot pepper flakes or similar spice

½ head of escarole, thinly chopped

Ground black pepper

Directions

Preheat oven to 425F.

Oil a baking tray and put the sausages in oven until cooked through and well browned.

Remove sausages from the oven, let them cool and then cut into chunks.

Add ½ cup of chicken stock to the baking tray and use a spatula to scrape off any browned pieces of sausage from the pan. You will use this later in the soup.

Take a large pot and place over a medium heat and add the olive oil.

Add the onions and sauté until translucent, usually this takes 3-4 minutes. Add the garlic and cook for further 1-2 minutes. Make sure they are well mixed.

Add the chicken stock (and the half cup of stock from the roasting pan), the beans, sausage chunks and pepper flakes.

Bring to the boil and then turn heat down and let it simmer for 30 minutes.

Whilst the soup is simmering away beautifully, chop your escarole. Add this to the soup and stir.

Cook for a further 20-30 minutes stirring occasionally. The escarole should start to break apart slightly and separate. If the soup begins to look too thick, add more stock.

Spicy, Roasted Chicken Tenders

Ingredients

¼ teaspoon grated lemon zest

1.5 tablespoon lemon juice

1 tablespoon garlic, finely chopped or minced

0.5 teaspoon dried oregano

1 tablespoon finely chopped jalapeno peppers

1 tablespoon olive oil

Sprinkle of salt

½ pound of chicken tenders, or breasts sliced lengthwise.

1 bell pepper, seeds removed and thinly sliced

½ onion, thinly sliced

Directions

Preheat oven to 425F.

Mix together the lemon zest, lemon juice, garlic, oregano, jalapenos, oil and salt in a bowl.

Add the chicken, pepper and onion to the bowl and toss to coat thoroughly.

On a baking tray spread the chicken tenders out evenly and cover with foil.

Bake for about 25 minutes, or until the chicken is cooked through.

Mackerel & Beetroot Salad

Ingredients

1 mackerel fillet

1 bag of salad leaves

1.5 beetroots chopped into chunks

¼ cup of pomegranates

2 teaspoons red wine vinegar

2 tablespoons extra-virgin olive oil

Juice and grated zest from 1 half of an orange

Sea salt, to taste

Ground black pepper, to taste

Directions

Place a pan over a medium heat and add 1 tablespoon of oil.

Heat the oil and then add the fish skin side down. Leave it to cook whilst you make the dressing.

In a bowl add the vinegar, remaining oil, orange zest and juice and the beetroot. Toss well.

Microwave this bowl until the beetroot is cooked and warmed through.

Add the salad leaves and pomegranates to the bowl and toss everything well.

After the mackerel has cooked for 5 minutes skin side down. Flip it and cook for a further 2 minutes, or until done. Fish should flake easily with a fork.

Lay the salad and beetroot on a plate and place the fillet on top of it. Drizzle any remaining sauces or juices over the dish as dressing.

Green and Mean Salad

Ingredients

2 cups of broccoli

½ cup of quinoa, cooked and cooled

2 avocados, stone and skin removed, chopped into chunks

1 cup of rocket leaves

2 tablespoons extra-virgin olive oil

1 teaspoon mustard seeds

1 teaspoon caraway seeds

150g sunflower seeds

150g pumpkin seeds

3 tablespoons sweet chilli sauce

1 lemon, for dressing

Directions

Cook the broccoli in a pot of boiling water.

Once cooked drain and set aside to cool

In a large bowl add all the remaining ingredients, except the lemon, and toss well.

When ready to eat squeeze the lemon over the dish.

Eat cold.

Nicoise Salad

Ingredients

2 eggs

1 can of tuna

Handful of green beans, chopped

Handful of cherry tomatoes, halved

1 cup of spinach, pressed

2 tablespoons low-fat mayonnaise

3 tablespoons balsamic vinegar.

Ground black pepper, to taste

Directions

In a pot of water add the eggs and bring to a hard boil. Once cooked, drain and set aside.

In a bowl mix together the beans, tomatoes, spinach, 2 tablespoons of vinegar and toss well. Set aside.

Mix the tuna with the mayo, pepper and remaining balsamic. Set aside.

Remove the shell from the eggs and cut into slices.

Create a bed from the salad and grind more pepper over this. Place the tuna in the centre and place the egg slices along the side.

Tuna Stir Fry

Ingredients

1 can of tuna

1 grated carrot, skin removed first

1 courgette, cut into rounds

1 head of Broccoli, ripped or cut into small pieces

Handful of green beans

2 tablespoons light soy-sauce

½ teaspoon ground ginger

1 teaspoon red pepper flakes

1 tablespoon extra-virgin olive oil

3 tablespoons of water

Directions

Place a wok over a medium-high heat and add the oil.

Add the green beans and broccoli to the pan and cook for 2 minutes, stirring continually.

Add the water and leave until it starts to steam.

Add the tuna, courgette and carrot. Mix well and cook for a minute, stirring continually.

Sprinkle the ginger and pepper flakes in and toss everything well. Continue until broccoli falls off a fork when stabbed. Should take a few minutes.

Take off the heat and drizzle with soy sauce.

Dinner Recipes

Scallop & Vegetable Kabobs

Ingredients

5 oz. scallops, enough for 2-4 skewers

1 tablespoons extra-virgin olive oil

Juice from half of a lemon

½ teaspoon thyme

2 shallots, peeled and halved

2 bell peppers, cut into chunks

6 cherry tomatoes

½ zucchini, cut into rounds

Ground black pepper, to taste

Sea salt, to taste

Skewers, soaked in water

Directions

In a bowl combine the oil, lemon juice, thyme, salt and pepper. Mix well and then add the scallops to this mixture and coat well. Leave to sit in this marinade for 20 minutes.

Whilst you marinade the scallops preheat your broiler/grill.

Skewer the vegetables and scallops in an alternating fashion.

Season with salt and pepper.

Place under grill and cook for about 2-3 minutes per side.

Beef Chilli Verde

This will cook enough for several portions, store in refrigerator for up to 1 week

Ingredients

1 tablespoon extra-virgin olive oil

1 onion, sliced

2 chilies, seeded and chopped

1 bell pepper, chopped

1 jalapeno, stem removed and chopped

1.5 lbs of stewing meat cut into cubes, roughly an inch in size

1 can of cannellini beans, drained

6 tomatillos with the husks removed, chopped

5 small chopped green chilies

4 cloves of garlic, finely chopped

1 cup of chicken broth

¼ teaspoon thyme

2 teaspoons oregano

2 teaspoons cumin

½ teaspoon ground black pepper

1 teaspoon rock salt or sea salt

1 tablespoons yellow cornmeal

Directions

In a large pot add the olive oil, chopped onion, 2 chilies, bell pepper and cook on high until the onion begins to turn translucent. Should take 3-5 minutes.

Add the beef and brown lightly. Stirring frequently.

Add the rest of the ingredients to pot and stir.

Bring everything to a boil and then switch the heat to low and simmer for 8 -9 hours.

Season with salt.

Quinoa

Ingredients

1 cup of quinoa

2 cups of vegetable stock

1 teaspoon of minced garlic

1 bay leaf

Ground black pepper, to taste

Sea salt, to taste

1 cup of chopped halved cherry tomatoes

Juice and zest from 1 lime

1 cup of chopped cucumbers

Half of an onion, chopped

1 bell pepper, chopped

Directions

Add the quinoa to a large pan and add the stock, garlic, bay leaf, pepper and salt. Bring to a boil with a medium heat.

Turn the heat down and let simmer for 15 minutes. Stirring occasionally.

Take off the heat and let it sit for minutes.

Fluff the quinoa with a fork.

Add the vegetables and herbs. Toss until mixed well.

Season with salt and pepper.

Mediterranean Inspired Chicken

Ingredients

2 chicken breasts

2 tablespoons sun dried tomatoes, chopped

2 tablespoons feta cheese, crumbled or torn

2 tablespoons black olives, stones removed and chopped

1 teaspoon of minced garlic, or finely chopped

1 tablespoon pine nuts

1 tablespoon balsamic vinegar

1 tablespoon extra-virgin olive oil

Directions

Preheat oven to 350F

In a bowl toss together all ingredients except for the chicken breasts.

Slice the chicken along the side creating a pocket in the breast. Don't cut the whole way through.

Place the stuffing inside the chicken.

Lay on an oven proof dish, drizzle with more oil and bake for 15 minutes.

Lean Chilli

This recipe makes enough for 3-4 servings. Can be kept in refrigerator for up to a week.

Ingredients

500g extra-lean minced beef

2 tablespoons minced garlic

4 teaspoons paprika

2 teaspoons cayenne

1 onion, chopped

1 can of kidney beans

1 can tinned tomatoes, chopped

1 tablespoon red pepper flakes

2 cups pressed spinach

1 tablespoon extra-virgin olive oil

Directions

Put a large pot over a medium heat and add the oil.

Once the oil is heated add the onion and half of the garlic. Cook for 5 minutes.

Add the beef and cook until well browned. Stirring frequently.

Add the tomatoes, kidney beans, pepper flakes, paprika and cayenne. Stir well.

Turn the heat to low and cook for 20 minutes. The sauce should have thickened by this time.

Turn off the heat add the spinach and stir in.

Cover and let sit for 1-2 hours.

Chilli Baked Salmon

Ingredients

2 salmon fillets

3 tablespoons sweet chilli sauce

1 red onion, chopped

1 garlic clove, finely chopped

1 courgette, sliced lengthwise

Directions

Preheat oven to 350F

Layer the bottom of an oven proof dish with chopped onion, garlic and courgette.

Place the salmon fillets on top and drizzle sweet chilli sauce over everything.

Cover and bake for 15-20 minutes.

Serve with green vegetables

Jerk Seasoned Chicken

Ingredients

2 Chicken breasts, sliced

1 tablespoon of jerk seasoning

3 red onions, sliced

1 cup of chicken stock

1 cup Quinoa

1 head of broccoli, cut or torn into small pieces

1 tablespoons of extra-virgin olive oil

Directions

Place the chicken and seasoning in a sealable bag and seal. Massage the bag gently to season the chicken and then let it marinate for one hour.

Cook the quinoa, as per package instructions, in the chicken stock.

Place a pan over a medium heat and add a tablespoon of oil.

Add the chicken, onion and broccoli to the pan and cook for 5 minutes.

Drain the quinoa and put on a plate. Add the contents of pan onto the top and any juices left in the pan use as a dressing.

Turkey Meatball Chilli

This will make enough for at least 3 portions. Keep in the fridge for up to a week.

Ingredients

500g turkey mince

1 teaspoon chilli flakes

1 teaspoon cayenne

2 tablespoons olive oil

1 egg, whisked

Ground black pepper, to taste

2 teaspoon minced garlic

2 cans of kidney beans

2 cans of tinned tomatoes, chopped

2 tablespoons of yoghurt, flavourless

Directions

In a large bowl add the turkey, chilli, cayenne, pepper and 1 teaspoon of garlic. Mix well using your hands and then add the egg.

Form the meat into balls. Be careful not to press together too tightly.

Place a deep pan over a medium heat and add the oil before gently adding the meatballs. Cook until well browned on all sides.

Remove meatballs and set aside.

Keeping the heat on medium add the tomatoes, remainder of the garlic, yoghurt, pepper, kidney beans and stir well. Bring the sauce to a boil before turning the heat to low.

Add the meatballs back to the pan and mix everything together.

Cover and cook on low for 30 minutes.

Seafood Linguine

Ingredients

Handful of gluten-free linguine

1 teaspoon of minced or finely chopped garlic

4 cherry tomatoes, quartered

2 egg yolks

1 can of tinned crab meat

1 handful of frozen shrimp

3 tablespoons extra-virgin olive oil

2 teaspoons red pepper flakes or dried chilli flakes

Ground pepper, to taste

Directions

Cook the linguine in a pot, according to instructions on package.

Whilst the linguine cooks place a pan over a medium heat and add 1 tablespoon of oil.

Add the tomatoes, shrimp, pepper flakes and garlic to the pan and stir well. Cook for 3 minutes, stirring frequently, before adding the crab meat and egg yolks.

Cook for another 2 minutes, stirring continually.

Drain the linguine and add to the pan. Toss well.

Drizzle the remainder of the oil on the pasta and season with pepper.

Protein Paella

Ingredients

Chorizo, 6 ½ cm thick rounds

Chicken breast, chopped into small pieces

Handful of frozen shrimp

Handful of mussels, still in shell

1 teaspoon minced garlic

1 onion, chopped finely

1 cup of paella rice

1 red pepper, chopped

½ teaspoon of saffron, optional

¾ cup of chicken stock

½ cup of frozen peadss

1 tablespoon olive oil

Ground black pepper, to taste

Salt, to taste

Directions

In a wok, or deep pan, add the oil and heat it over a medium heat.

Add the chorizo and chicken pieces and cook for 5 minutes, or until chicken is cooked through. Set aside.

Add the pepper, onion and garlic to the pan and cook for 4-6 minutes. Keep the ingredients moving in the pan.

Add the rice to the pan and toss well. Let cook for 2 minutes, stirring continually.

Pour in the stock and add the saffron, if using. Bring to the boil stirring once or twice before lowering the heat and covering. Cook until the rice is thoroughly cooked, should take 20 minutes or so.

The stock should be fully cooked off now. Add the chorizo, chicken, seafood and peas to the pan. Increase the heat to medium and cook for a further 7 minutes.

Season with pepper and salt.

Steak Salad

Ingredients

1 steak, the choice of cut is up to you

1 onion, sliced

1 bag of salad leaves

3 tablespoons balsamic glaze

1 tablespoon extra-virgin olive oil

Ground black pepper, to taste

Sea salt, to taste

Directions

Add the olive to a pan and place over a high heat.

Once the pan begins to smoke add the steak and onions. Sear each side of the steak for 1-2 minutes before turning heat down to medium.

Cook the steak to your liking. When cooked turn off heat and let steak rest for 3 minutes in the pan.

Whilst the steak cools take a large bowl and mix your salad leaves and cooked onions with the balsamic glaze.

Take the steak from the pan and slice into thin pieces.

Toss with the salad leaves. Any leftover juices in pan should be used to dress the salad.

Season with salt and pepper.

Veggie Burger

Ingredients

½ can of black beans, drained

½ bell pepper, cut into small pieces

½ onion chopped into wedges

2 garlic cloves, peeled

1 egg

1 tablespoon chili powder or chilli flakes

1 tablespoon cumin

1 teaspoon hot sauce

¼ cup bread crumbs

Directions

Preheat oven to 380F. Lay baking tray with parchment paper.

Mash together the black beans until they form a thick paste

Add the pepper, onion and garlic to a food processor and pulse for 10 seconds. Stir in mashed black beans.

In a bowl whisk together the egg, chilli powder, cumin and hot sauce. Add this to the bean mixture.

Mix in the bread crumbs and mix well. Form 2 large patties.

Bake for 15 – 20 minutes. Or until burger is cooked through the middle.

Place on burger buns and serve however you like.

Garlic Baked Tilapia

Ingredients
2 tilapia, fillets

2 cloves garlic, crushed or finely chopped

3 tablespoon extra-virgin olive oil

1 onion, finely chopped

1 tablespoon cayenne pepper

Salt and Pepper, to taste

Directions
Lay the fish fillets in an oven proof dish. Rub them well with the crushed garlic.

Drizzle with the olive oil until well coated. Evenly lay the onion across the fillets.

Cover and refrigerate overnight or at least 6 hours.

Preheat oven to 350F

Remove fish from oven. Sprinkle with cayenne, salt and pepper. Let fish come to room temperature, about 30 minutes.

Bake for 30 minutes.

Honey Ginger Salmon

Ingredients

2 individual small salmon fillets

1 red onions, finely chopped

1 garlic clove, minced

1 teaspoon olive oil

2 tablespoon honey

2 teaspoon grated ginger

1 teaspoon hot sauce

Directions

Preheat oven to 350F.

Using 1 tablespoon of oil, coat an oven proof dish.

Lay the salmon fillets on this, surround with the onion and garlic.

Sprinkle the ginger and hot sauce over everything. Drizzle the honey evenly over the fillets.

Bake for 20 minutes.

Flaked Fish in Lemon Lentils

Ingredients

2 oz. Lentils, Puy are best

½ onion, finely chopped

½ carrot, finely chopped

1 celery stick, finely chopped

½ pint vegetable stock

1 tablespoon half-fat crème fraiche

1 tablespoon chopped dill

The zest of ½ a lemon

1 white fish fillet

Handful of baby spinach

Directions

Add lentils into an oiled pan with the chopped onion, carrot and celery and place over a medium heat.

Add the stock and bring to the boil. Stir a few times and reduce the heat. Cover and let simmer for 20-25 minutes. The lentils should be tender after this time.

In a bowl mix together the crème fraiche, half the dill and the lemon zest, adding a little seasoning, to taste.

Put the fillets in a shallow microwave proof dish with a splash of water and cover with cling film leaving one corner open slightly.

Microwave on medium for 4-6 minutes until the fish flakes easily when touched with a fork. Flake the fish with a fork.

Once the lentils are tender, add the spinach and stir. Continue to cook at a low heat and add the crème fraiche once the spinach has wilted.

Serve and top with flaked fish. Garnish with the remaining dill.

Rosemary & Garlic Chicken

Ingredients

2 chicken breasts

2 teaspoons minced garlic

2 tablespoons of rosemary

1 tablespoon lemon juice

Salt and pepper to taste

Directions

Preheat oven to 375F.

Lay chicken breasts in an oven proof dish and season with other ingredients.

Cover the dish and back for 25 minutes, or until cooked through.

Sides Recipes

Cauliflower Mash

Ingredients

1 head of cauliflower, stem removed

½ tablespoon of red pepper flakes

Ground black pepper, to taste

Sea salt, to taste

Directions

Add the cauliflower heads to a microwave safe bowl and add 1 inch of water.

Cover and microwave for 2 minutes, or as long as need to cook. The cauliflower should fall off a fork when stabbed.

Drain the water. Microwave again for 1 minute.

Add the seasoning and mash the cauliflower using a fork or masher.

Greens for Any Dish

Ingredients

1 head of Broccoli, cut or torn into pieces

1 handful of green beans

1 cup of spinach, pressed

1 half of a courgette cut into rounds

1 tablespoon of minced garlic, or finely cut

½ tablespoon cayenne pepper

2 tablespoons extra-virgin olive oil

Ground black pepper, to taste

Sea salt, to taste

Directions

Place a deep pan over a medium, heat the olive oil and garlic.

Add the broccoli and green beans and cook for 5 minutes, stirring frequently.

Add the courgette and cayenne pepper. Cook for 2 minutes, stirring frequently.

Add the spinach and cook until it is wilted. Ensure everything is folded together.

Grind pepper and sprinkle salt to taste.

Need More Carbs?

Ingredients

1 tin of kidney beans, black beans or lentils, drained

½ cup of medium/hot salsa

Ground black pepper

Directions

Add everything to a microwave safe bowl, cover and cook until ready

Baked Sweet Potato

Ingredients

1 sweet potato, washed

1 teaspoon garlic, minced

1 teaspoon paprika

1 tablespoon extra-virgin olive oil

Directions

Preheat oven to 350F

Stab multiple holes in your sweet potato using a fork and microwave for 10 minutes.

Cut the potato in half and stab more holes on each face. Microwave for 5 minutes.

Cut the potato halves in half again so you know have quarters. If the potato isn't soft yet microwave again.

Line a baking tray with foil and place potato pieces on them. Sprinkle with garlic and paprika before drizzling the oil on top.

Bake for 15 minutes, or until crispy on top

Stuffed Mushrooms

Ingredients

2 large cap mushrooms

¼ cup of tomato puree

½ Goat's cheese, torn or crumbled

Ground black pepper, to taste

Directions

Preheat oven to 350F

On a baking tray bake mushrooms for 5 minutes, underside up

Remove from oven and cut or scoop out the underside. Add to a bowl.

Add the tomato puree to the bowl and mix well. Generously add pepper.

Stuff this mixture back into the mushroom caps and return to oven for 7 minutes.

Add the goat's cheese on top of the mixture and cook for a further 2 minutes.

Kale Chips

Ingredients

Bag of kale

Sea Salt

Ground black pepper

2 tablespoon extra-virgin olive oil

Directions

Preheat oven to 350F

Lay kale chips on baking tray. Season with olive, salt and pepper.

Bake until crispy.

All rights Reserved. No part of this publication or the information in it may be quoted from or reproduced in any form by means such as printing, scanning, photocopying or otherwise without prior written permission of the copyright holder.

Disclaimer and Terms of Use: Effort has been made to ensure that the information in this book is accurate and complete, however, the author and the publisher do not warrant the accuracy of the information, text and graphics contained within the book due to the rapidly changing nature of science, research, known and unknown facts and internet. The Author and the publisher do not hold any responsibility for errors, omissions or contrary interpretation of the subject matter herein. This book is presented solely for motivational and informational purposes only.

Image: Creative Commons "Get Abs, Get Volume, Get Paid" by Next TwentyEight under CC. Image edited by Author.

Printed in Great Britain
by Amazon